Made in United States
Troutdale, OR
08/11/2023

11980972R00064